LEADERSHIP RESTORATION

STOP MANAGING BACKWARDS, START LEADING FORWARD

MARY D. AUGUST-ANDERSON

authorHOUSE®

AuthorHouse™
1663 Liberty Drive
Bloomington, IN 47403
www.authorhouse.com
Phone: 1-800-839-8640

Published by AuthorHouse   01/20/2015

ISBN: 978-1-4969-5786-3 (sc)
ISBN: 978-1-4969-5787-0 (e)

Library of Congress Control Number: 2014921911

Table of Contents

Leadership: Taking Another Look

Finding balance from the top of the organization; leading vs. managing.

WHY I WROTE THIS MANIFESTO

I have a passion and purpose for changing lives of others. Through this manifesto, I seek to assist those with a desire to reach their designed purpose. My interest is to develop first time leaders (Self-titled, supervisors, and managers). Of course, being a leader does not always encompass a formal title.

I have grown exhausted of the many genres of deceptive (in my opinion) leadership in the world today. However, I will keep this discussion focused on personal and professional leadership within the workplace environment.

Are you overwhelmed with defective and or ineffective leadership? Here's what I know for sure, ineffective leadership will cast at least one of the below characteristics, if not all. (Just to name a few)

Broken promise (if it ever really existed)
Favoritism
Denied promotion
Unfairness
Inconsistent

SPECIAL ACKNOWLEDGEMENT & DEDICATION

There are many individuals that I give special acknowledgement and dedication to because I have many lessons learned. As we all may know, every lesson learned is not learned equally from positive or negative experiences, but perhaps from more of one than the other; served as an impartation of where I am today, respectfully!

Rather mentioning names, I thank each individual that has or had a season in my life which resulted into a worthy experience and ultimately helping me to reach my designed purpose. This manifesto on leadership and development is just the beginning of what is yet to come. I furthermore and explicitly dedicate the power and knowledge within this manifesto to God and my partnership with the John Maxwell Team. My future is being impacted by this relationship and I am extremely grateful. Additionally, I give dedication to my life line supporters; you know who you are.

MY TRUTH AS I KNOW IT

God Bless and enrich each individual, group, and organization that read, relate, and gain from this manifesto.

A few undeniable truths; there is a distinct difference between leading others versus managing others. More often than not, teams are being managed rather than lead. How do we make a difference?

Do you consider yourself a leader? Lay aside any formal titles, look in the mirror and ask yourself, "Am I leading or managing?" Go ahead, find the definition of both and discover the two opposites.

I discovered within myself more managing than leading and I have always considered myself to be a leader by definition, but realizing that I was managing more; this was an eye opening day of awareness. There must be a healthy balance of leading and managing whether you are in the workplace or simply the leader of your family. When there is balance there is progress, when there is progress there is growth, when there is growth, there is success.

You may be asking, "How did this happen?" My experience was handed down from one leader to the next. When I think of each individual that had a role throughout my professional career; the styles of management were all based more on managing teams rather than true leadership development.

Let's break the cycle!

As a career professional in the health care industry for more than twenty years, I have experienced many changes, including management, leadership styles, witty, and charming personalities (or not) to go along with it. As years pass, people, policies, procedures, and technologies change; improving the way we conduct business and transition during the process. However, often times in this transition someone is left behind, including those holding a position of leadership (as titled) because of unwillingness to change or learn, usually. *This will undoubtedly limit leadership growth for the leader as well as their team.*

What I have experienced; the easier way to convey information of change is by *managing* it forward, to the front line. My question to you, "How better would your organization perform if top Executives (i.e. CEOs, VPs, Sr. Executives, etc.) were to balance leadership and managing? Versus only managing a team and passing this forward. If any organization expects consistent results, then stop managing backwards and start leading forward from the top, not the bottom up (i.e. Front line staff); find an equal balance. This type of imbalance is demonstrated within many organizations where front line staff are "managed information" and expected to achieve results (not necessarily in vain), but when this is not being balanced (leading and managing) and required or executed at every level; employee satisfaction, morale, customer satisfaction, and organizational goals are impacted. Therefore, an organization's potential is minimized.

I want to live in a world where leaders are not afraid.

I want to live in a world where leaders are not intimidate

I want to live in a world where leaders are willing *to share the wealth of knowledge, respectfully!* To those that want to receive.

Let's break the cycle!

LEADERSHIP VS. MANAGING

Many will be able to attest to the differences of leading and managing. Is there room for both?

As mentioned early on and according to many descriptions and definitions there are a few distinct differences for the words lead and manage. There are a couple of definitions and descriptions that resonated with me and how I performed with my teams on a daily basis. To be a leader one must guide (direction); showing the way, influence, and inspire. Another definition expounded on leaders focusing first on the achievement of others rather than self. This reminds me of a quote, "It's amazing what you can accomplish if you don't care who gets credit" – H Truman.

I believe that many are familiar with the saying, "Get out of your own way". How would the performance of your team improve if you removed yourself (what you get from it) and focus relentlessly on the achievement of your team members?

Another view of managing is to dominate or influence someone by tact, flattery, or craftiness. When you are *managing* your team, there is a constant battle of control and handling rather than effective influence when *leading* your team. Managing only can become a form of dictatorship and less influential (positively). As leaders, the importance of balancing both (lead and manage) is detrimental to the health and performance of your team and organization.

In my opinion, this goes without saying, but I will say it anyway. It is easy to just manage because you are simply relying on telling someone else what to do. The real work comes in when you begin to lead. Once the two are combined, this means that you are comfortable with "the leader in you" and you are learning who your team members are individually and collectively because as a leader – you would know *through your leading abilities* that no one team member can be *managed* in the exact same manner.

Let's break the cycle!

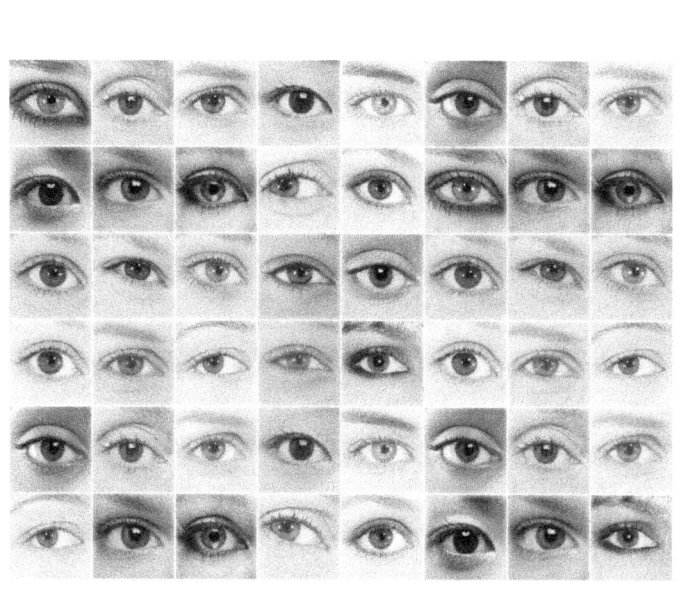

AN INTRODUCTION TO THE I'S OF LEADERSHIP

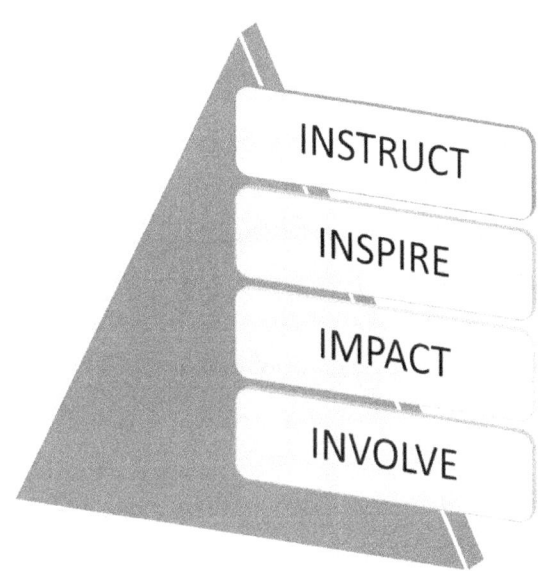

INSTRUCT

INSPIRE

IMPACT

INVOLVE

- INSTRUCT

Instruct may sound impersonal in a sense when thinking of a leadership role. Although, each of us perform as leaders at any given time whether professional or personal. In doing so, instructions are passed on at some point. How can a leader instruct and lead simultaneously?

As a leader, teaching is instructing; (show and tell) someone what, how, and when to do something. Truth be told, most of us are waiting to be told or shown what to do in life anyway. If you or someone you know is seeking an opportunity to become a millionaire, what do you think their or your question would be? "How do I..."What do I..."When do I... And the answer to whatever one may be seeking is a well-developed plan by someone showing or instructing (teaching and leading) you on how to reach that sought after desire; methodically providing knowledge, information, and or skill to others.

Let's conclude that to **instruct** is simply to teach!

- INSPIRE

Inspire can be viewed or defined as leading. To inspire, you are guiding and encouraging others to follow (whoever or whatever the desire may be). Inspiration in my opinion, is a feel-good terminology. As a leader, one should be in a position to inspire or make others feel excited, proud, successful, and encouraged. How can you inspire your team or an individual to their next level in business or life? One of my favorite quotes and in my opinion is truth when you are a leader. "A leader is one who knows the way, goes the way, and shows the way" – John C. Maxwell

- IMPACT

Impact is to make a difference. How can you make a difference with others? To impact is to influence, to influence is to follow, and to follow is to lead. If you are a leader in any capacity, do you have followers? If you have no followers, you are not leading! Influence is powerful and necessary whether you are leading in a professional or personal capacity.

Make the decision to **impact** others' lives today!

- INVOLVE

Involve is being in partnership with your team. Include your team with different aspects of decision-making, developing activities and or initiatives of improvement within the organization, etc. Engage with your team and allow them to engage with each other. Involvement builds relationships, relationships build trust and together with many hands, many minds, and one goal, success is accomplished. Teamwork indeed does make the dream work.

Get your team **involved** and engaged!

COMMUNICATING AS LEADERS

Well, there is not any need for a defined explanation because the word communicate literally speaks for itself. Although, this is probably a large cause for many unsuccessful practices and relationships of all kind.

Communicate, communicate, and communicate.

Communication is one of the most pivotal actions needed to sustain any relationship, professional or personal. Lack of communication will be detrimental to any relationship and as mentioned, will result to unsuccessful outcomes. Effective communication is important when leaders convey organization and department goals.

How much better would your team perform and excel with effective communication? Here are three substantial standards that make good leadership sense given by my mentor from his "A daily devotional" by John C. Maxwell to guide you as you lead and communicate to your team:

❑ **Be Consistent** – This is probably one of the biggest complaints among employees where they have experienced inconsistencies and sometimes lack of decision making with their respective management teams. Do not expect consistency of your team if you as a leader are not consistent.

❑ **Be Clear** – Your team cannot successfully execute if they do not know what to do. Impress them with straight forwardness (clear and concise information). Do not dazzle your team with your intelligence.

❑ **Be Courteous** – Everyone deserves respect no matter your position or title. If you are courteous, you set the tone for your organization and your team.

THE WAY I SEE IT, WHAT NOT TO DO AS A LEADER

This is probably an arguable topic; what **not** to do as a leader. I am going to list a few that you may simply agree to disagree (or not), but as you read along, grab a mirror and take an assessment. Adhere to the reality of your findings and make a difference.

As a leader, please do not…

Take your team for granted
Be unfair
Be inconsistent
Be rude and selfish
Show a lack of concern
Discourage growth
Breech confidentiality and trust
Support negativity
Overlook future leaders
Overlook strengths and weaknesses
Waist time, energy, and resources with habitual slackers (recognize the difference)
Forget about development

Let's break the cycle!

STOP MANAGING SDRAWKCAB
Sᴛᴀʀᴛ Lᴇᴀᴅɪɴɢ ꜰᴏʀᴡᴀʀᴅ

Follow me:

Facebook, LinkedIn

Websites:

www.johnmaxwellgroup.com/
maryanderson

www.writtenbydzine.wordpress.com

Booking Events:

Personal Coaching, Team training, and Teaching

Individual and group sessions

Mastermind groups

Contact email:

mary.starcouturetravel@gmail.com

www.ingramcontent.com/pod-product-compliance
Lightning Source LLC
Chambersburg PA
CBHW071828170526
45167CB00003B/1466